Wonderful Counselor, Prince of Pea

Lion of Judah, Lamb of God, The G

Sure Foundation, The Resurrection

The Vine, Christ, The Lord of Host

The Word of God, Man of Sorrows,

Bright Morning Star, Wonderful C

Prince of Peace, Lion of Judah, L

Lamb of God, Sure Foundation, The

The Vine, Crist, The Lord of Hosts

The Word of God, Man of Sorrows,

Morning Star, Wonderful Counselor,

o Prince of Peace, Lion of Judah, L

Lamb of God, The Good Shepherd, T

The Wisdom of God, Sure Foundation

onderful Counselor, Prince of Peace,
ion of Judah, Lamb of God, The God
ure Foundation, The Resurrection, Th
he Vine, Christ, The Lord of Hosts,
he Word of God, Man of Sorrows, B
Bright Morning Star, Wonderful Cou
rince of Peace, Lion of Judah, Lam
amb of God, Sure Foundation, The
he Vine, Crist, The Lord of Hosts,
he Word of God, Man of Sorrows, B
orning Star, Wonderful Counselor,
Prince of Peace, Lion of Judah, Lam
amb of God, The Good Shepherd, The
he Wisdom of God, Sure Foundation,

The NAME ABOVE ALL NAMES

UNWRAPPING THE NAMES *of* JESUS

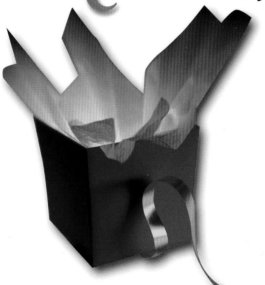

Jane L. Fryar

www.ctainc.com

Scripture quotations are from The Holy Bible, English
Standard Version, copyright © 2001 by Crossway Bibles, a
division of Good News Publishers. Used by permission.
All rights reserved

ISBN 0-9728816-4-6

PRINTED IN THAILAND

THE NAME ABOVE ALL NAMES

UNWRAPPING THE NAMES *of* JESUS

I magine an eighteen-wheeler rumbling down your street, a fantastic logo emblazoned on its side. Picture it maneuvering to park just inches from the curb outside your house. Hear a SWOOSH as the driver sets the air brake, and then watch as he swings his body out the cab door and plants his boots on the road below. See him stride up your sidewalk, carrying a clipboard with its sheaf of papers. Listen, as your doorbell announces his arrival.

It's here! An unexpected shipment! And it's come to you, direct from the world's preeminent supplier of extravagant gifts. How long would it take you to sign the bill of lading and throw open your front door to receive it?

Jesus – God's Gift of Grace

Unwrapping the Gift celebrates an even more thrilling gift – a magnificent gift chosen personally for you. It's a gift designed to bring you more pleasure and comfort than anything you could imagine, as well as meet more of your practical needs than anything you've seen. It's God's gift of grace in our Savior, Jesus, and it lies totally outside the realm of our experiences on earth. In fact, the apostle Paul used terms of another dimension when he described this gift in a letter to the ancient Ephesians.

For us, everything seems to exist in 3-D; our universe appears three dimensional – built around the dimensions of length, width, and height. But Paul was inspired to acknowledge other dimensions; he prayed that God would give us strength *"to comprehend with all the saints what is the breadth and length and height and depth, and to know the love of Christ that surpasses knowledge, that you may be filled with all the fullness of God"* (Ephesians 3:18-19).

Did you catch it? The love of Christ, which Paul articulated, has four dimensions! Simply put, that love surpasses our ability to wrap our minds around it! And one thing's for sure – no truck, garage, or home here on earth will hold it. This gift can only be housed in human hearts.

EMPTY HEARTS, LONGING TO BE FILLED.
HEARTS FULL OF QUESTIONS
                    OR CONCERNS
                        OR CONFUSION
                            OR CONVICTION.
EXPECTANT HEARTS, EAGER FOR LOVE'S TOUCH.

Do not restrain your enthusiasm, for your heavenly Father rejoices when his children rip off the wrapping paper of his exquisite love with the excitement and impatience of a six-year-old on Christmas morning! *(See Zephaniah 3:17.)*

That's the truth! God the Holy Spirit is beside you right now, ready to expand your heart's capacity to receive all the benefits he intends to pour into your life through Jesus – His gift to you!

NAMES, NAMES, AND MORE NAMES

Individuals born to royalty here on earth customarily inherit many names and titles. Great Britain's Prince Charles, for instance, is known officially as:

His Royal Highness Prince Charles Philip Arthur George, Prince of Wales, KG, KT, GCB, AK, QSO, PC, ADC, Earl of Chester, Duke of Cornwall, Duke of Rothesay, Earl of Carrick, Baron of Renfrew, Lord of the Isles and Prince and Great Steward of Scotland.

Today, titles such as these remain mostly ceremonial, but at one time they indicated definite and concrete roles, responsibilities, and rights belonging to the title-holder.

In Scripture we meet the Royal Son of God, ascribed literally by dozens of names and titles. Far from meaningless formalities, each of these names and titles describes definite and concrete roles, responsibilities, and rights that belong to God's Son. What's more, our Lord intends to bless us through each and every one of these names and titles. Scripture promises, *"those who know your name put their trust in you"* (Psalm 9:10). Such is the power and beauty of each name.

Each chapter in this book unwraps one of these glorious names or titles. As you read, let the Holy Spirit enlarge your understanding of who Jesus is and what he has done on your behalf! Let your growing appreciation of God's gift evoke trust and true worship in your heart.

This gift is so big we will spend eternity trying to take it all in. Beginning today, enjoy the fullness of the life you were meant to live; select any name in this book and receive that life as it has been given you. Many, many blessings and much encouragement await you.

JESUS

MATTHEW 1:1, 21; TITUS 1:4

Imagine this headline: "Baby Saves the World!" Can you conjure up a set of circumstances in which this headline could possibly be legitimate? (The tabloids don't count!) What would such a baby have to do? Somehow bring together two warring superpowers? Wail in distress to distract a crazed dictator with his finger on the button, ready to launch a dozen missiles, each tipped with multiple nuclear warheads?

Any scenario we concoct seems far-fetched, to say the least. And yet, Matthew and Luke, the two Gospel writers who detail our Lord's birth and infancy, both make claims about a baby born to save the world. Both call the baby Jesus.

[A]n angel of the Lord appeared to [Joseph] in a dream, saying, "Joseph, son of David, do not fear to take Mary as your wife, for that which is conceived in her is from the Holy Spirit. She will bear a son, and you shall call his name Jesus, for he will save his people from their sins."
~ Matthew 1:20-21

And at the end of eight days, when he was circumcised, he was called Jesus, the name given by the angel before he was conceived in the womb.
~ Luke 2:21

JESUS, SAVIOR

A powerful metaphor lies embedded in each of the many names Scripture gives our Lord. But because we use the name Jesus again and again and again, we tend not to notice the word picture in which it is rooted. Jesus means Savior. The name evokes a rescue from extreme or deadly danger:

• A savior rushes into the operating room to perform such delicate, life-saving surgery that no other doctor on earth could attempt it. The patient lives, re-knitted and whole.

• A savior rappels down a cliff wall to rescue a hiker clinging to a spindly bush on a ledge only three-inches wide. The hiker grabs hold of him, glad to be pulled free from imminent death.

• A savior steps between a convenience store clerk and a drug-crazed robber holding a sawed-off shotgun. The clerk escapes to a tear-soaked reunion with loved ones.

The sick patient, the endangered hiker, and the threatened clerk all owe their lives to a savior. Keep them in mind as you mull over each Scripture below. How does each encourage you in the salvation or rescue that Jesus, your Savior, has worked for you?

> *[Jesus came] to give knowledge of salvation to [God's] people in the forgiveness of their sins ...*
> ~ Luke 1:77

> *For God has not destined us for wrath, but to obtain salvation through our Lord Jesus Christ...*
> ~ 1 Thessalonians 5:9

> *But I am afflicted and in pain; let your salvation, O God, set me on high!*
> ~ Psalm 69:29

> *O Lord, my Lord, the strength of my salvation, you have covered my head in the day of battle.*
> ~ Psalm 140:7

> *And I heard a loud voice in heaven, saying, "Now the salvation and the power and the kingdom of our God and the authority of his Christ have come, for the accuser of our brothers has been thrown down, who accuses them day and night before our God."*
> ~ Revelation 12:10

Some of Christianity's most enduring hymns carry the name Jesus in their titles and expand upon the rescue he has achieved. Think about the words of the hymn on the next page as you worship your Savior, Jesus, now.

ALLELUIA!

SING to JESUS!

Alleluia! Sing to Jesus!
    His the scepter, his the throne.
Alleluia! His the triumph, his the victory alone.
Hark! the songs of peaceful Zion
    thunder like a mighty flood.
Jesus out of every nation
    has redeemed us by his blood.

Alleluia! Bread of heaven,
    here on earth our food and stay!
Alleluia! Here the sinful
    flee to you from day to day.
Intercessor, Friend of sinners,
    earth's Redeemer, plead for me.
Where the songs of all the sinless
    sweep across the crystal sea.

~ William Chatterton Dix, 1867

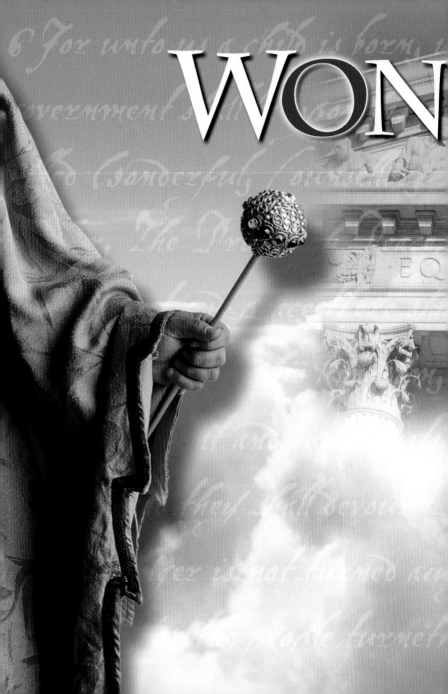

WON

DERFUL
COUNSELOR
ISAIAH 9:6

An old television ad shows a customer's eyes glazing over when, at the end of the day, a grocery clerk forces one last decision: Paper? Or Plastic? Most of us laughed when we first saw the ad. Psychologists call it "the laughter of recognition." After all, we've stood in that customer's shoes! But whether decisions are easy or difficult, they have a way of crowding into our lives.

† Should I buy this house, that condominium, or continue to rent?
† Should I add fries or a salad to that burger?
† Should I invest in a new car or keep riding the bus?

† Should I book a window or an aisle seat for next week's flight to Boston? Or take the train? Or stay home?

Each day we make trivial decisions – and momentous ones! We value our freedom, but sometimes, especially when difficult decisions crowd us, pushing and prodding, our hearts half-hope that someone will tell us what to do, will take over our responsibilities for personal decision-making.

WISE COUNSEL

If you've been a parent or worked as a teacher, you understand the process children experience as they develop the ability to make sensible decisions. Few parents permit a three-year-old to decide whether or not he needs a coat on a cold winter's morning. Few teachers allow 13-year-olds to decide whether or not to do this week's math assignments.

However, wise parents do ask, "Do you want to wear the blue shirt or the purple shirt to preschool?" Likewise, perceptive teachers encourage 13-year-olds to experiment with assignment notebooks and study schedules to determine which works best for them. Children who grow up without the opportunities and freedom to make decisions and, ultimately, the opportunities and freedom to make mistakes, rarely reach their most creative and productive potential.

God, our heavenly Father, established this grow-to-your-potential principle. Therefore, although he holds us

accountable to the firm boundaries he set in the Ten
Commandments, he seldom dictates the directions in which
we move. You will not read "Buy the green beans" engraved in
the ice on your grocer's frozen food case. God simply does not
control every move at every crossroads.

Jesus is a "Wonderful Counselor," not a Commanding
General. He came to enhance our freedom and inspire our
humanity, not to remove or diminish them. As counselor, he
gives us true wisdom whenever we ask for it. His counsel
instills in us the courage and hope we lack in our frightening
and distressing world.

The prophet Isaiah first penned the prophecy promising
that the coming Savior would be for us a "Wonderful
Counselor" (Isaiah 7:14). Later in his book, Isaiah makes this
promise to God's repentant people:

> *[The LORD] will surely be gracious to you at the sound
> of your cry. As soon as he hears it, he answers you.*
>
> *And though the Lord give you the bread of adversity and
> the water of affliction, yet your Teacher will not hide
> himself anymore, but your eyes shall see your Teacher.*
>
> *And your ears shall hear a word behind you, saying,
> "This is the way, walk in it," when you turn to the right
> or when you turn to the left.*
> ~ Isaiah 30:19-21

What a beautiful picture of the gracious, gentle work our Teacher does for us and in us! Even in adversity, even in affliction, our Wonderful Counselor never deserts us. He never throws up his hands in disgust at our weakness or sin. He never walks away from us.

KNOWING AND DOING GOD'S WILL

So how does the Lord Jesus guide, advise, and direct us? He does this primarily, of course, through his Word. As we continue to read, study, and meditate on the Scriptures, our Teacher sits beside us. As we listen to our pastor preach, our Teacher opens our eyes, our ears, and, most importantly, our hearts. As we continue to ponder his truths, our Teacher shapes our thought processes and our emotions so that we gain his perspective regarding the situations and circumstances of our lives.

Slowly, but surely, we begin to think as he thinks; we begin to see what he sees; we begin to feel the way he feels. We even begin to believe what he says is true. Slowly, but surely, our decisions and actions reflect those of our Lord more than those of our culture. This transformation occurs as we look to Jesus for counsel, offering our open hearts to his truth:

> *Do not be conformed to this world, but be transformed by the renewal of your mind, that by testing you may discern what is the will of God, what is good and acceptable and perfect.*
> ~ Romans 12:2

Will we ever reach a point at which perplexity vanishes? Will we ever have such perfect intuition that we can stick to the Highway of Holiness and avoid the Thicket of Confusion and Bog of Disobedience?

No. We will not make perfect decisions or live perfectly until we enter heaven. Yet he does begin the process of transformation within us the moment we become Christians, the moment his Spirit enters our lives. God has promised to put *"his Spirit in our hearts as guarantee [of what is to come]"* (2 Corinthians 1:22).

As we look expectantly to Jesus, he removes the veil of despair and misunderstanding. Jesus frees us to behold and believe his wondrous truth: *"When one turns to the Lord, the veil is removed … there is freedom … and we all, with unveiled faces, beholding the glory of the Lord, are being transformed … from one degree of glory to another"* (2 Corinthians 3:14-18).

Jesus continually brings our understanding to maturity, making it possible for us to recognize, cherish, and follow his will as he aligns our hearts and minds with his.

What perplexities do you face today? What decisions weigh heavily on your heart? Just think, for exactly times like these God's gift to you is a Wonderful Counselor - a Teacher - in the person of his very own, dearly loved Son. Ask now for his comfort and counsel and then receive it by his grace.

PRINCE
of PEACE

ISAIAH 9:6

Without seeing the magnificence of the royal palace, one can never sense the dignity of the emperor.

So wrote a Chinese poet who lived during the seventh century Tang dynasty. A millennium later, Chinese rulers took the poet's observation to new heights as they created and furnished the complex that became known as the Forbidden City. Deep in the center of the capital and isolated from ordinary people, emperor after emperor in the Ming and Qing dynasties carried out affairs of state and mastered the politics of power from the opulent halls and lavish courtyards of the Forbidden City.

A BLOODSTAINED THRONE

Contrast the luxury and power of human monarchs with that of the Savior, the Prince of Peace. No deed to an earthly palace lay guarded in his vault. No keys to a throne room dangled from his belt. He once told his would-be courtesans:

> *The kings of the Gentiles exercise lordship over them, and those in authority over them are called benefactors. But not so with you. Rather, let the greatest among you become as the youngest, and the leader as one who serves. For who is the greater, one who reclines at table or one who serves? Is it not the one who reclines at table? But I am among you as the one who serves.*
> ~ Luke 22:25-27

Our Prince's service began in Mary's virgin womb. That service carried him in infancy to a rough, wooden manger. His service matured in a backwater village of a powerless people in Galilee. And it culminated on a cross.

Jesus came, not to lord his royalty over his human creatures, but to save them, to serve them. Our Prince ascended to blood-soaked Calvary rather than to a throne! And, he publicly took upon his own holy heart the punishment our sin and guilt deserved instead of isolating himself in the luxury of some forbidden, heavenly city. He is our Prince of Peace. Our Servant King.

TURMOIL AND UNREST

Two professors sat talking at Starbuck's across the street from a large university. The conversation grew more and more animated until one of them threw his arms open wide, sending two cups of cappuccino careening halfway across the table. "All I want is some peace!" he exclaimed. "Where can I go to get some peace?"

Sometimes, we Christians answer a question like this by suggesting Jesus as the source of peace. Of course, it's true. But if we boldly and lovingly offer Jesus to a troubled world, while neglecting to mention the all-important cross on which he sacrificed himself, we've boldly and lovingly doomed that world. We fail to connect the dots. We paint only half the picture. Certainly, Jesus brings peace. He is, as Scripture testifies, the Prince of Peace.

Still, Scripture quite specifically asserts that Jesus made *"peace by the blood of his cross"* (Colossians 1:20, *emphasis added*). This same text plainly diagnoses the root source of our restlessness, our dis–ease; it says that all human beings were *"once … alienated [from God] and hostile in mind, doing evil deeds"* (v. 21).

Can the relationship between human beings and the holy God really have degenerated that far? Can our minds truly hold that much hostility? Can our deeds be genuinely evil? The Bible says yes. And whether we feel it to be so or not, Scripture does not lie.

† We may not have murdered anyone, but, undoubtedly, we have demeaned others in angry or insulting words – if only in our hearts. Jesus taught that in the eyes of God, one such attack is as bad as murder. (See Matthew 5:21-26.)

† We may not have committed adultery, but it's likely we have entertained lustful thoughts. Jesus taught that in the eyes of God, one is as bad as the other. (See Matthew 5:27-30.)

† We may give regularly to the needy, but if we do it with mixed motives, to gain the reputation of a generous person, decrease our tax liability, or simply because it makes us feel bighearted, Jesus calls us hypocrites. (See Matthew 6:2.)

† We may show great affection toward our friends, but Jesus taught that we must demonstrate love for our enemies, praying for them and looking for ways to do good toward them. (See Matthew 5:43-48.)

While many claim to adhere to Jesus' instructions for godly living described in what's known as Christ's Sermon on the Mount, no one is able to do so. Taken from that sermon, these four examples show that no human heart is "perfect even as [our] Father in heaven is perfect" (Matthew 5:48). The guilt this reality evokes discourages, depresses, and deflates us. It stresses the heart, creating in it restlessness and alienation.

GOD'S GIFT: PEACE

B ut while Scripture diagnoses the source of our restlessness and alienation, it also points the path to the peace that can soothe it. That path runs through Calvary where Christ Jesus, the Prince of Peace, was hanged, "enthroned," as it were, in love for us – for you and for me:

> *God was reconciling the world to himself in Christ, not counting men's sins against them.*
> ~ 2 Corinthians 5:19

> *And you, who once were alienated and hostile in mind, doing evil deeds, he has now reconciled in his body of flesh by his death, in order to present you holy and blameless and above reproach before him…*
> ~ Colossians 1:21-22

Once we are "holy and blameless and above reproach" in God's eyes, we enjoy a peace no person or position or power on earth can give. Jesus promised this:

> *Peace I leave with you; my peace I give you. I do not give to you as the world gives. Do not let your hearts be troubled and do not be afraid.*
> ~ John 14:27

Such relief, this peace that flows from the throne of God! It's his gift to you, wrapped in swaddling cloths and lying in the Christmas manger!

LION of JUDAH

REVELATION 5:5

King Richard the Lion-Hearted. What pictures does this name conjure up for you? King Richard's nickname evokes banners emblazoned with a scarlet lion and snapping in the morning sun. Precursors to flags in later centuries, banners like this often flew over battlefields long ago.

King Richard probably had such a banner, and it no doubt did sport a lion. Why? Even those of us who dozed our way through Western Civilization in high school or college understand that a ruler with the nickname "lion-hearted" must have set his people an example of courage and confidence.

PRAISE AND COURAGE

Our Lord Jesus lived the life of a simple peasant here on earth. He led no conquering troops into battle. So why does Scripture call him the "Lion of Judah" (Revelation 5:5)?

The roots of this name grow deep in Scripture, grow all the way into the bedrock of the Bible's first book, Genesis. In Genesis, we see an aged Jacob blessing each of his 12 sons, sons whose descendents will go on to form the 12 tribes of Israel. Jacob took special pains as he pronounced his final blessing on his fourth-born son, Judah. Prophetically, Jacob knew that the Promised One, the Messiah, would come from the line of Judah. Accordingly, these words stand out from Jacob's blessing:

Judah is a lion's cub;
  from the prey, my son, you have gone up.
He stooped down; he crouched as a lion
  and as a lioness; who dares rouse him?
~ Genesis 49:9

Who dares rouse him, indeed! From early in Israel's history, God's people knew that their deliverer would come as a powerful, conquering lion. Also, from that time, the tribe of

Judah held a prominent, symbolic place in Israel's nationhood. Its symbolism speaks to us today about gifts our God has given us in this our Savior, heaven's Lion.

Judah's name sounds like the Hebrew word for praise. As the nation camped in the wilderness before entering the Promised Land, God directed that Judah pitch its tents on the east side of the camp, toward the rising sun. Each day for 40 years as the nation set out toward its new home, the tribe of Judah raised its banner and marched out first. This, too, happened at God's explicit command. (See Numbers 2:2-9 and 10:11-16.)

Can you see, then, that the Lion – Judah – led the way into each new day? Can you imagine the people of God moving forward into each of those days, into their future, praising the Savior God who had rescued them? Can you envision God's people laying aside their fears and following the banner of the Lion, praising him for his mighty love? That is exactly the blessing the Lord wanted for his people.

And if you can see all that, can you put yourself in the picture? Do you march under the banner of the Lion – the Lion of Judah? You can! You can face your own future, day-by-day, with the same courageous confidence, no matter what it holds. No matter what it holds! That is exactly the blessing the Lord wants for you!

If you wonder about that, consider that the course of Israel's early life as a nation did not always run smooth. Its people had to battle their way into the inheritance God had promised them. Their bumps and potholes and enemies and battles correspond in many ways to our own. They often stumbled as a people, sometimes badly. But the Lion never left their side.

He stood guard, defending and encouraging them in his love and forgiveness for them.

Do you trip over life's potholes? Do you stagger in daily ruts of temptation or fear or discouragement? Do you feel alone, abandoned to your fate? You need not! The mighty Lion of Judah never leaves your side! He's gone ahead of you, preparing the way. He even passed through the doorway of death itself to make the way safe for you! Because of Christ's cross and open tomb, you need never battle by yourself in fear and frustration. Instead, you can rely fully on your conquering, lion-hearted, resurrected Lord!

THE LION'S ROAR

Our universe began as Judah's Lion simply spoke the stars and planets and galaxies into existence. Imagine the day when that Lion will roar! His roar will shout the universe into a new existence:

The LORD roars from Zion,
  and utters his voice from Jerusalem,
  and the heavens and the earth quake.
~ Joel 3:16

And I saw the holy city, new Jerusalem, coming down out of heaven from God, prepared as a bride adorned for her husband. And I heard a loud voice from the throne saying, "Behold, the dwelling place of God is with man . . . ."
~ Revelation 21:2

On that day, *"The Lion of the Tribe of Judah will take the scroll of judgment and open its seals"* (Revelation 5:5). On that day, the day of our liberation, all God's people will return to him the mighty hymn of praise that rightly belongs to him as the Lion of Judah, the Lamb of God:

> *Worthy are you to take the scroll and to open its seals, for you were slain, and by your blood you ransomed people for God from every tribe and language and people and nation, and you have made them a kingdom and priests to our God, and they shall reign on the earth.*
> ~ Revelation 5:9-10

The Lion of the tribe of Judah, the Root of David, has conquered evil (Revelation 5:5)! He is our refuge, our stronghold. In his name we lift up our banners and walk into our future with confident hope. This assurance is God's gift to us, a gift wrapped in the tiny baby of Bethlehem.

The next day John seeth
saith, Behold the Lamb of

LAMB of GOD

JOHN 1:29

March comes in like a lion and goes out like a lamb. From New England to the Midwest and on toward the Rocky Mountain states, this old wives' tale proves itself true year after year. The icy rain and wild winds of March 1 contrast sharply with the soft breezes and warm sunshine of March 31.

Lion. Lamb. The two create quite a contrast. So, too, is the contrast between the Lion of Judah and the Lamb of God.

SHEEP TO THE SLAUGHTER

When a lion roars, every creature on the plains of the Serengeti takes notice. Some reports have the sound of such a roar carrying up to five miles! A sheep bleats, and who notices? (Only the lion if, of course, he is hungry!)

What are we to make of the Bible's contrasting portraits of Jesus?

> † He's the Lion of Judah. He's the Lamb of God.
> † He's King of all and Servant of all.
> † He's majestic and humble.
> † He wields great authority and acts in perfect meekness.
> † He's courageous, but compassionate.
> † He's mighty, but so very gentle.

The prophet Isaiah foretold the Lamb's humility, meekness, compassion, and gentleness:

He was oppressed, and he was afflicted,
  yet he opened not his mouth;
like a lamb that is led to the slaughter,
  and like a sheep that before its shearers is silent,
  so he opened not his mouth.
By oppression and judgment he was taken away;
  and as for his generation, who considered
that he was cut off out of the land of the living,
  stricken for the transgression of my people?
And they made his grave with the wicked
  and with a rich man in his death,
although he had done no violence,
  and there was no deceit in his mouth.
~ Isaiah 53:7-9

Incredible strength under complete control. That's the sense of the word gentleness as it applies to our Lord Jesus. The apostle John tells us that when the temple guards came to arrest Jesus in Gethsemane, they "fell to the ground" at his mere word (John 18:6). Jesus himself had earlier asserted, *"No one takes [my life] from me, but I lay it down of my own accord. I have authority to lay it down, and I have authority to take it up again. This charge I have received from my Father"* (John 10:18).

Still, despite his ability to defend himself, Jesus went to the cross for our sins "like a lamb … led to the slaughter," just as Isaiah had prophesied. Not under any compulsion, except of course, the compulsion of compassion, of love.

BEHOLD, THE LAMB OF GOD!

The Old Testament consistently portrays the coming Messiah as a lamb destined for slaughter. The entire sacrificial system God gave Moses on Mt. Sinai foreshadowed the coming of the Lamb of God. Ancient Israel knew that all the blood of all the animals they offered for all those centuries could not wash away sin, could not cleanse human guilt. Instead, it showed the need for a final sacrifice; it pointed forward to Jesus, the spotless Lamb, who removed the sin of the world on a single day – the Friday Christians call "good." (See Zechariah 3:9.)

John the Baptizer could have been pointing to Christ on Calvary when he shouted for all to hear:

"Behold, the Lamb of God, who takes away the sin of the world!"
~ John 1:29

Here is God's gift to you – the perfect sacrifice that has removed your guilt, all your guilt, forever!

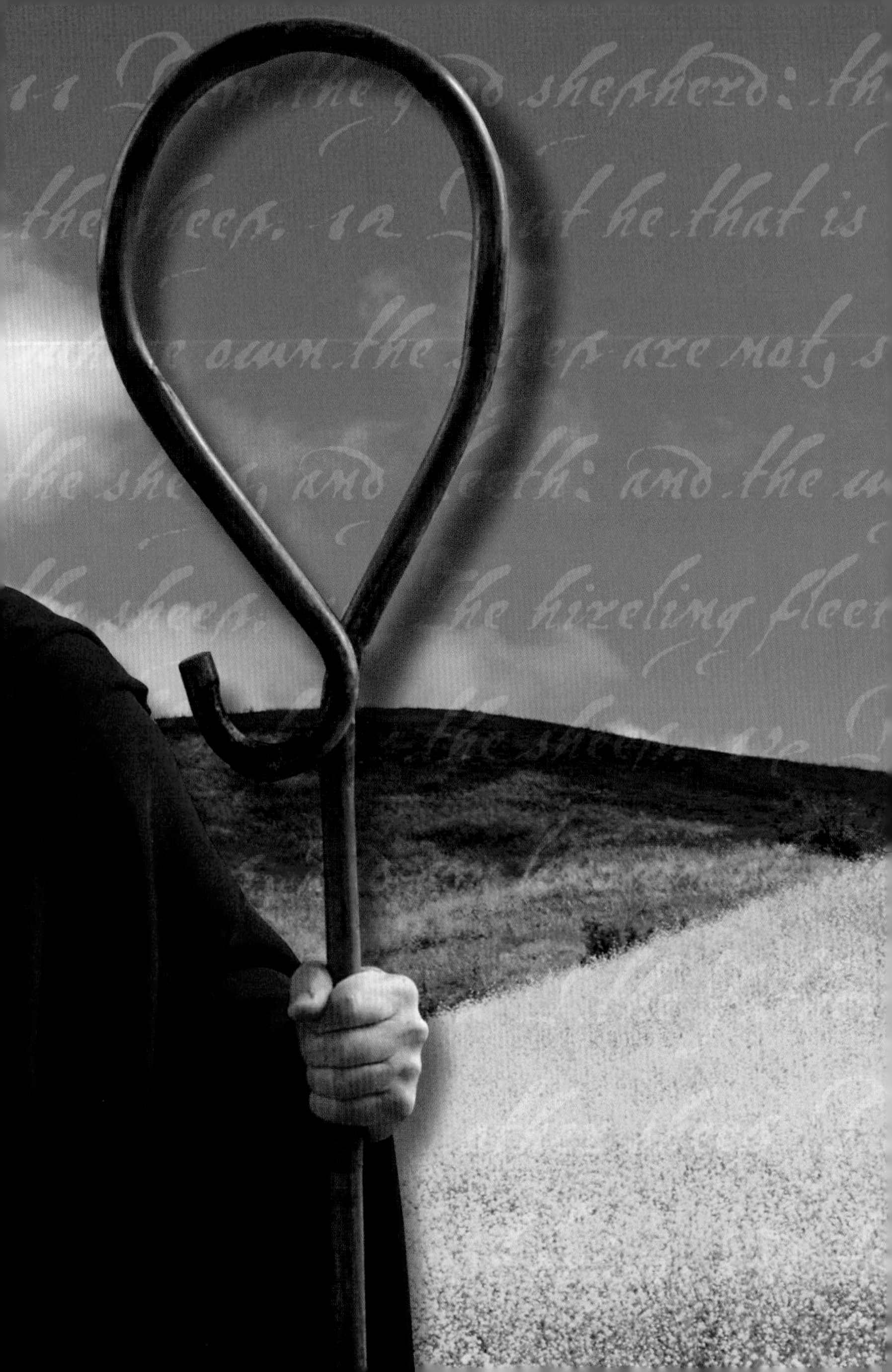
shepherd:
he that is
own, the
are not
and the
hireling

GOOD SHEPHERD
JOHN 10:11

Beloved. It's the only word to describe the scripture passages that portray Jesus as our Good Shepherd:

The Lord is my shepherd; I shall not want.
He makes me lie down in green pastures.
He leads me beside still waters.
He restores my soul …

The familiar words of Psalm 23 soothe and calm us, no matter how frazzled our day or how many hassles we've untangled. We long for those green pastures. We crave those waters of rest.

Jesus applies this imagery to himself in the familiar, and similarly beloved, words of John 10:

> *I am the good shepherd. I know my own and my own know me, just as the Father knows me and I know the Father; and I lay down my life for the sheep. And I have other sheep that are not of this fold. I must bring them also, and they will listen to my voice. So there will be one flock, one shepherd.*
> ~ John 10:14-16

How does Jesus shepherd us? What can we count on from our Good Shepherd? The apostle Peter gave several hints as he defined the role of Christ's "under shepherds," the elders who pastor today's congregations in our Lord's name:

> *Shepherd the flock of God that is among you, exercising oversight, not under compulsion, but willingly, as God would have you; not for shameful gain, but eagerly; not domineering over those in your charge, but being examples to the flock. And when the chief Shepherd appears, you will receive the unfading crown of glory.*
> ~ 1 Peter 5:2-4

Like Jesus the Good Shepherd, those who care for God's people are to do so willingly, eagerly, and tenderly, just as Jesus, the chief Shepherd, does.

WILLING AND EAGER

The sun baked the meadow like an oven. All day long, the sheep bleated in complaint, wanting more of the shade and water so hard to come by in this part of their range. All day long, the shepherd tended them. One yearling buck tried to wander off four times. In his final jaunt, he skidded down an embankment to land under a prickly bush near a patch of inedible weeds.

The shepherd saw him, poised precariously at the top of the hill one minute and gracelessly somersaulting over it the next. As the shepherd trotted over the rise to the rescue, he also skidded on some stones and fell headlong, landing near the yearling's bush. His knees and palms stung as he dusted them off and picked up his reckless lamb.

Late in the afternoon, the flock followed the shepherd to the sheep pen. Sweaty and hungry, he could almost feel the cool water he would soon splash over his face and neck. His stomach growled as he imagined the aroma rising from the supper he would prepare over the campfire. Ten more minutes, and comfort would settle over his tired body.

But as his little flock reached the pen and started through its gate, the shepherd sensed something wrong. He stared harder into the twilight. Sure enough, the yearling was missing. Again.

His heart pounding, the shepherd hurried the rest of the sheep into the pen, latched the gate, and rushed back down the path, toward the meadow. His fatigue forgotten, he raced in his thoughts back through the day. Where had the yearling gone? "I must find it!" he thought to himself.

Would you forgive this yearling and its foolishness? Would you willingly leave your own supper and shower to search for it? How many times could you answer yes to these questions?

Jesus shepherds us willingly, even eagerly. He did what it took to rescue us from sin and death. He did it, not resentfully, but in love. Jesus is our willing Savior, eager even now to help us in every time of need!

TENDER

With twilight nearly gone and darkness falling fast, the lamb lay, barely breathing, beneath a rocky ledge far from the path. It heard the crunch, crunch, crunch of sandaled feet moving slowly along the gravel on the trail. The footsteps stopped as the shepherd looked toward the ledge, looked away, and looked back again. "Something there?" he murmured to himself. "Or not … ."

The lamb had no strength left to bleat. Nonetheless, the shepherd took a step in its direction. Paused. Then took another. By the third step, the shepherd was running toward the ledge and the mangled body that lay beneath it.

Tears filled the shepherd's eyes as he saw the damage – a bone protruding through the skin of one leg, an eye swollen shut, and blood-caked wool below gashes that had bled too long and threatened to reopen if provoked even slightly.

The shepherd stripped off his jacket, and as tenderly as he knew how, picked up the limp body and wrapped the jacket around it. Taking up the bundle in his arms, he set out for home, walking as urgently – and as gently – as he could through the gathering darkness.

Would you feel so tender, so merciful toward this runaway? Would you take such care to avoid causing more pain? Would you focus on the lamb's needs rather than your own as you planned your next steps?

Jesus did. His tender compassion toward you will overwhelm your heart when you begin to understand it. The impenitent and the ungodly hear only words of woe and condemnation from Jesus' lips. But the broken-hearted hear his love. Your Good Shepherd tenderly cares for every hurting, repentant heart. He stands before you right now, ready to forgive and heal, even when the wounds are self-inflicted.

Remember and cling to his words:

I am the good shepherd. I know my own and my own know me, just as the Father knows me and I know the Father; and I lay down my life for the sheep. And I have other sheep that are not of this fold. I must bring them also, and they will listen to my voice. So there will be one flock, one shepherd.
~ John 10:14-16

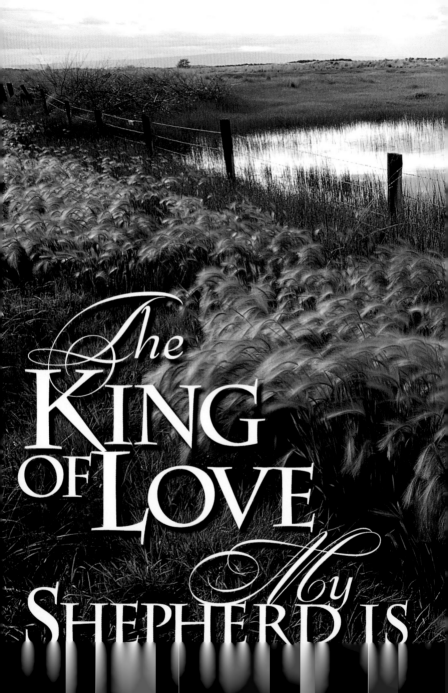

The KING
OF LOVE
My
SHEPHERD IS

The King of love my Shepherd is,
Whose goodness faileth never,
I nothing lack if I am his
And he is mine forever.

Where streams of living water flow
My ransomed soul he leadeth,
And where the verdant pastures grow,
With food celestial feedeth.

Perverse and foolish oft I strayed,
But yet in love he sought me,
And on his shoulder gently laid,
And home, rejoicing, brought me.

In death's dark vale I fear no ill
With thee, dear Lord, beside me;
Thy rod and staff my comfort still,
Thy cross before to guide me.

Thou spread'st a table in my sight;
Thy unction grace bestoweth;
And O what transport of delight
From thy pure chalice floweth!

And so through all the length of days
Thy goodness faileth never;
Good Shepherd, may I sing thy praise
Within thy house forever.

~ Henry W. Baker, 1868

The WISDOM of GOD

1 CORINTHIANS 1:24

Early in the twentieth century, psychologists and educators worked to develop a test that could gauge human intelligence. By 1910, the Stanford-Binet test was being widely administered to determine the Intelligence Quotient (IQ) of individuals. Those with "average" intelligence scored about 100 on the Stanford-Binet test, or so its proponents claimed.

A decade or so after IQ tests came into widespread use, social scientists began to speculate about the IQ of historic figures, most of them dead for decades or even centuries. By studying information about their childhoods, and by considering the work they left behind, various "experts" began to publish lists ranking the IQ's of philosophers, scientists, and other prominent individuals. One well-publicized list included these scores:

† Goethe, German poet and scholar: 210.

† Pascal, French mathematician: 185.

† Isaac Newton, English scientist: 180.

† John Calvin, Swiss theologian: 175

Thankfully, the name of Jesus Christ appeared on none of these lists. Most scholars at that time realized such speculation would offend Christians, seeming disrespectful or even blasphemous. But consider these questions:

† Does Jesus Christ understand nuclear energy?

† Or microwave ovens?

When asked, a surprising number of Christians answer "No" to questions like these! Why? Maybe because we think of Jesus as a resident of first century Palestine, losing sight of who he, in truth, is – the Creator of the universe, of all that exists:

> *[Christ] is the image of the invisible God, the firstborn of all creation. For by him all things were created, in heaven and on earth, visible and invisible, whether thrones or dominions or rulers or authorities – all things were created through him and for him. And he is before all things, and in him all things hold together.*
> *~ Colossians 1:15-17*

While physicists continue to explore the forces that keep atomic nuclei together and that keep our universe from flying apart, we can read the apostle Paul who tells us clearly, "In [Christ] all things hold together."

CAN'T OR WON'T?

Imagine a "god" who wanted to help us hold our lives together, who wanted to help with our problems, fears, or needs – but couldn't do it. Or didn't know what to do! A god like that might resemble the Wizard of Oz, hiding the secret of his impotence behind a curtain, fearful of the day that those who come to him for help discover the fraud. Rightly, Dorothy called this kind of wizard a "humbug."

The gift our heavenly Father gave the world in Jesus is no humbug! Our Lord Jesus, the prophet tells us, is "the Mighty God" (Isaiah 9:6). Consider these descriptions:

> *And to him [Christ] was given dominion*
> *and glory and a kingdom,*
> *that all peoples, nations, and languages*
> *should serve him;*
> *his dominion is an everlasting dominion,*
> *which shall not pass away,*
> *and his kingdom one*
> *that shall not be destroyed.*
> ~ Daniel 7:14

> *Great and amazing are your deeds,*
> *O Lord God the Almighty!*
> *Just and true are your ways,*
> *O King of the nations!*
> *Who will not fear, O Lord,*
> *and glorify your name?*
> *For you alone are holy.*
> *All nations will come*
> *and worship you,*
> *for your righteous acts have been revealed.*
> ~ Revelation 15:3-4

Is Jesus powerful? Absolutely! He wields absolute power. What's more, he is the Wisdom of God incarnate, wiser than Solomon himself:

> *[Jesus said,] The queen of the South will rise up at the judgment with this generation and condemn it, for she came from the ends of the earth to hear the wisdom of Solomon, and behold, **something greater than Solomon is here**.*
> ~ Matthew 12:42, emphasis added

> *And on the Sabbath he began to teach in the synagogue, and many who heard him were astonished, saying, "Where did this man get these things? What is the wisdom given to him? How are such mighty works done by his hands?"*
> ~ Mark 6:2

Paul sums it up in these words: *"Christ the power of God and the wisdom of God"*
~ 1 Corinthians 1:24

CAN AND WILL

All-powerful. All-wise. Christ Jesus is both. In our need – whatever need we face – Jesus knows what to do, and he has the might to do it. Beyond even this is the blessed truth that he wants to help us, for Jesus is not only the wisdom and power of God, he is *"our righteousness and sanctification and redemption."*
~ 1 Corinthians 1:30

† Righteousness – On his cross, Jesus made us right with heaven's court, canceling the debt we incurred by our sins.

† Sanctification – On his cross, Jesus cleansed our hearts, purging away our sin and selfishness and giving us a new heart of love toward others.

† Redemption – On his cross, Jesus rescued us, offering up the ransom we could never pay and setting us free from our captivity to the powers of death and evil.

What gifts we received from our Mighty God! What gifts we received in our Mighty God! Who would believe the Wisdom of God could be hidden in such a tiny package – Bethlehem's baby boy!

SURE
FOUNDATION
ISAIAH 28:16

Soviet tanks rolled into the little village in the region of Silesia just as German tanks rolled out of it. It was 1945, and the village people were about to exchange one oppressive government for another.

The young pastor of the village church had no illusions about life getting better under Communism. He only prayed that he would be allowed to stay, to care for his people.

Try as he might, the military governor for the region could not dissuade the pastor from his foolish prayer. Nor could the committee of bureaucrats who eventually assumed governance in the village. In the end, they gave him a monthly stipend – something under $40 per month, and assigned him to look after the church building and grounds.

It was a pittance, even in that poverty-stricken pocket of Soviet rule. But for a while, the pastor was happy. He had his health, he led a handful of mostly older women in worship each Sunday, and he managed to hide his Bible from the secret police who visited from time to time. God had truly blessed him.

But one day, as he tried to enter the church, he had to push the door with all his might. It occurred to him that the door had opened less and less willingly for several months. As he walked around the corner to the back of the building, he gasped. A diagonal crack had opened in the brick wall. Suddenly, the crack that had appeared last week in the tile floor made sense.

The foundation was giving way. It did not take long to discover why. Replete with seams of coal, the entire region had gradually become honeycombed with underground mines. Now the miners had tunneled under the village, and the church's foundation could no longer support the weight that sat on it.

THE STABILITY OF OUR TIMES

Solid footing. Without it, the future holds only the specter of dust and rubble – for a building or a life. Scripture calls Jesus the only cornerstone, the sure foundation:

Thus says the Lord GOD,
"Behold, I am the one who has laid as a foundation
in Zion, a stone, a tested stone,
a precious cornerstone, of a sure foundation:
'Whoever believes will not be in haste.'"
~ Isaiah 28:16

Those who build their lives on this foundation, on Christ's unconditional love and on his *"precious and very great promises"* (2 Peter 1:4), enjoy life's only genuine stability. When tempests of trouble blow or torrents of temptation pour down, this Foundation will not give way. This Foundation will never collapse.

EVEN WHEN STEEPLES ARE FALLING

For more than 40 years the pastor of the little Silesian church propped up its structure, despite the crumbling foundation. More importantly, for 40 years, until the Soviet occupiers left the region for good, he struggled on, supported only by Christ as he comforted the sick, tended the dying, and encouraged God's people with the Good News of Christ, their one, sure Foundation. He refused to collaborate with the government. He would not betray those from the Christian underground who looked to him for leadership. He stood firm in *the faith once for all delivered to the saints*" (Jude 3).

For 40 years, Christ Jesus proved himself faithful in this man's life. The same Jesus will prove himself faithful in your life, too. He is your one, sure Foundation, no matter what threatens to topple your commitment to your Lord. He has promised:

> *[The LORD] will be the stability of your times, abundance of salvation, wisdom, and knowledge; the fear of the LORD is [your] treasure.*
> ~ Isaiah 33:6

...after you have suffered a little while, the God of all grace, who has called you to his eternal glory in Christ, will himself restore, confirm, strengthen, and establish you.
- 1 Peter 5:10

Restoration. Confirmation. Strength. Stability. These are God's gifts to you in Jesus, your Sure Foundation!

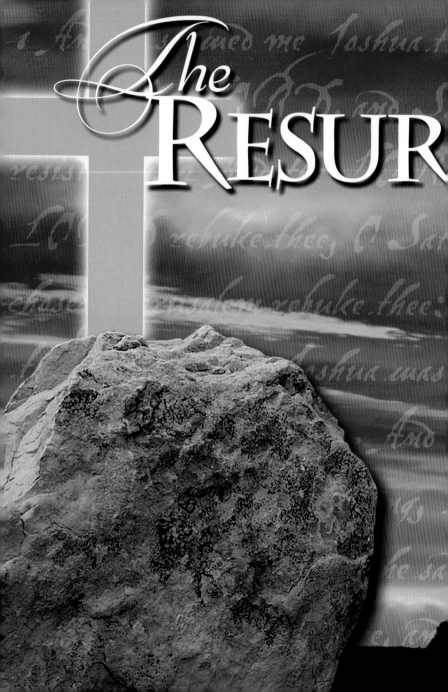

RECTION
JOHN 11:25

Athens. Holy Saturday. A few minutes before midnight in the year of our Lord, 790. The believers have been observing the Easter Vigil for hours. Their 40-day observance of Christ's suffering and death for every sin is about to end.

As 12:00 AM draws near, the city's Archbishop and all the priests exit the church. The king and queen join them on a raised platform above a waiting crowd. Everyone holds an unlighted candle. Few dare to breathe as they await the stroke of midnight and the jubilation it will unleash. The priests continue to chant a low, somber melody.

Then it happens! A single cannon booms in the distance, announcing the stroke of midnight. Easter Day has begun. The Archbishop lifts the cross high as he shouts, "Christos anesti!" Christ is risen!

At once, every person in the sea of believers waiting below repeats the good news. The shout rises and repeats again and again, triumphant and glorious: Christ is risen! Christ is risen!

In that same moment, darkness dissolves as flames pass from candle to candle, and light begins to flow like a mighty river in every direction. Drums roll and rockets flare into the sky. Hearts leap for joy as young and old exchange hugs of delight.

Still in our century, year after year, Holy Week continues to open into the Holiest Day believers know, the Holiest Day we ourselves will ever know. At different times and in different places the Church has celebrated Easter in different ways. But always, in every celebration, Christ's people have struggled to express the glory of the resurrection. Our words and songs of praise always fall short; the splendor of his victory far outshines our ability to praise him for it!

No ceremony. No song. No ritual. No spontaneity. No words. No exclamation. Nothing we can say or do or feel can fully capture the glory of the Resurrected One.

"I AM THE RESURRECTION"

Stand for a moment with Martha at the tomb of her brother, Lazarus. His body has lain in the tomb for four days. As you hear Jesus ask some bystanders to roll back the stone sealing the entrance, alarm fills your heart. As delicately as you can, you point out the obvious, "Lord, by this time the body stinks!"

Yet Jesus moves ahead with his intended miracle, reassuring you: Believe! You are about to see the glory of God! Moments later, the brother whom you had lost to death stands before you, very much alive. You hold him tight, your heart flooded with joy and your mind racing over the words of your Friend:

> *I am the resurrection and the life. Whoever believes in me,*
> *though he die, yet shall he live, and everyone who lives*
> *and believes in me shall never die. Do you believe this?*
> ~ John 11:25-26

Jesus could raise Lazarus because Jesus is the Resurrection. Just as the first crocus of Spring foreshadows flowering gardens, Lazarus signifies the millions of believers from all time and every place who will hear Jesus' voice and obey his command of grace: Come out! Jesus does not simply raise his people from death; Jesus is the Resurrection! He is the Life!

Every tear you have ever shed at every graveside during every loved one's funeral will be wiped away. Every fear that has ever set your heart pounding at every nasty diagnosis you have ever received from any doctor will evaporate. Jesus has pried death's bony grip off your throat!

Jesus is your Resurrection! Jesus is your Life!

No wonder Christians struggle to express the joy. The manger points to the cross. The cross lights the way to the open tomb. The tomb explodes into joy "inexpressible and filled with glory" (1 Peter 1:8)! What a gift!

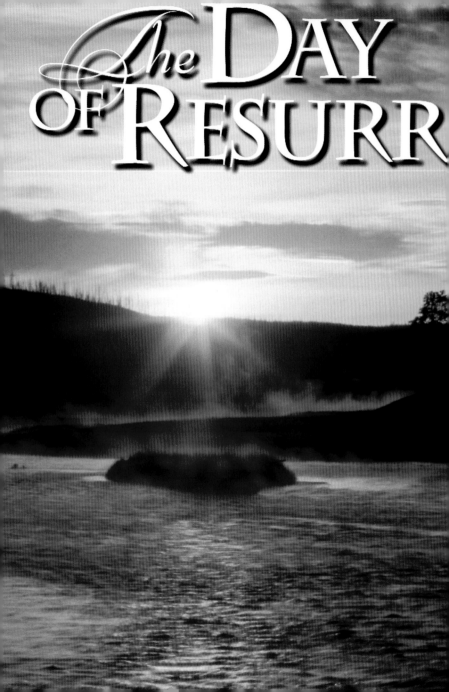

The DAY OF RESURR

ECTION

The day of Resurrection:
Earth! Tell it now abroad!
The Passover of gladness,
The Passover of God!
From Death to Life Eternal —
From this world to the sky —
Our Christ has brought us over,
With hymns of victory!

Now let the heav'ns be joyful!
Let earth its song begin!
Let the whole world keep triumph,
And all that is therein:
Invisible and visible
Their notes let all things blend —
For Christ our Lord has risen —
Our joy that has no end.

~ St. John of Damascus,
7th Century

OUR
ADVOCATE
ZECHARIAH 3:1-10

Imagine yourself at eight years old, picked on by a schoolyard bully. What a relief to know you have a big brother on the high school football team who will take your side!

Or imagine yourself at 28, facing charges for a capital crime. You begin to despair as you imagine your fate. What a relief to know that your big brother heads the nation's best law firm and that he has every lawyer and paralegal on his staff working day and night on your behalf!

NOT GUILTY!

When we cannot speak up for ourselves, when we don't know what to say or how to say it, we need a spokesperson. How much better when that person brings more than muscle to the conversation! How much better when our advocate truly cares about us and can offer persuasive arguments in our defense!

Jesus, our Defender, speaks on our behalf before the throne of God. The prophet Zechariah portrays our Lord Jesus, pleading our case:

> Then he showed me Joshua, the high priest standing before the angel of the Lord, and Satan standing at his right side to accuse him. The Lord said to Satan, "The Lord rebuke you, Satan! The Lord, who has chosen Jerusalem, rebuke you! . . ."
>
> Now Joshua was dressed in filthy clothes as he stood before the angel. The angel said to those who were standing before him, "Take off his filthy clothes." Then he said to Joshua, "See, I have taken away your sin, and I will put rich garments on you."
>
> Then … they put a clean turban on his head and clothed him, while the angel of the Lord stood by.
> ~ Zechariah 3:1-5

A cleansed and restored priesthood – that's the imagery here, the truth symbolized by "Joshua the high priest." You and I are that priesthood in Jesus, a holy priesthood:

But you are a chosen race, a royal priesthood, a holy nation, a people for his own possession, that you may proclaim the excellencies of him who called you out of darkness into his marvelous light.
~ 1 Peter 2:9

Jesus pleads our case; he stands by our side, answering every charge Satan, our Accuser, can muster against us. Not only that, Jesus paid our penalty – the death penalty! Now he drapes around our shoulders the royal robe of his righteousness, his holy life lived in our place. From head to toe, we stand before God clean, forgiven, free. The apostle John explained Jesus' on-going role:

My little children, I am writing these things to you so that you may not sin. But if anyone does sin, we have an advocate with the Father, Jesus Christ the righteous. He is the propitiation [payment] for our sins, and not for ours only but also for the sins of the whole world.
~ 1 John 2:1-2

ADVOCATE AND INTERCESSOR

B ecause we can claim Christ's righteousness, his right standing before heaven's courts, we also can petition that court when we have any other need. Jesus continuously takes our case, advocating on our behalf. Even when our need is so great or our problem so complex that we have no idea what to ask, Jesus intercedes for us:

> *Fear not because your prayer is stammering, your words feeble, and your language poor. Jesus can understand you. Just as a mother understands the first lispings of her infant, so does the blessed Savior understand sinners. He can read a sigh, and see a meaning in a groan.*
> ~ from J. C. Ryle, A Call to Prayer

Jesus loves to answer prayer. He loves to intercede for you! He has your best at heart and will see that you receive God's very best! Let the splendid gift of his advocacy fill your heart with thanksgiving and awe!

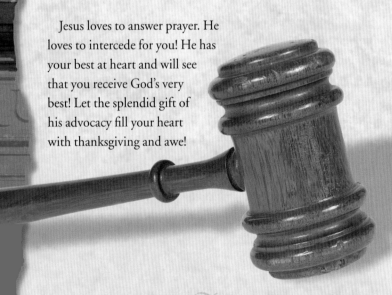

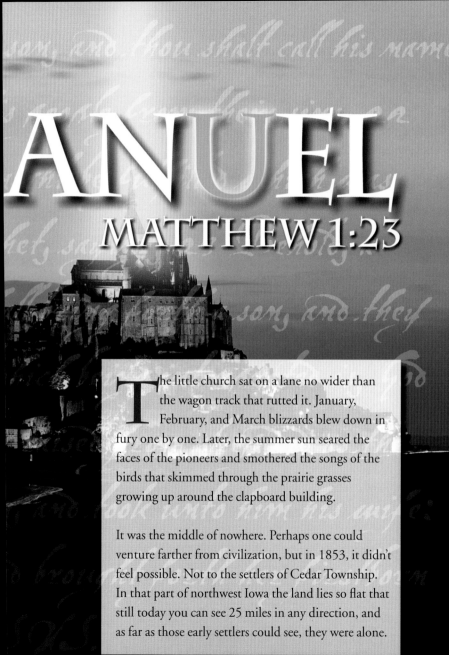

ANUEL

MATTHEW 1:23

The little church sat on a lane no wider than the wagon track that rutted it. January, February, and March blizzards blew down in fury one by one. Later, the summer sun seared the faces of the pioneers and smothered the songs of the birds that skimmed through the prairie grasses growing up around the clapboard building.

It was the middle of nowhere. Perhaps one could venture farther from civilization, but in 1853, it didn't feel possible. Not to the settlers of Cedar Township. In that part of northwest Iowa the land lies so flat that still today you can see 25 miles in any direction, and as far as those early settlers could see, they were alone.

Significantly, they named their new little church, Immanuel:

> *Behold, the virgin shall conceive and bear a son, and they shall call his name Immanuel (which means, God with us).*
> ~ Matthew 1:23

"Despite all appearances, we are not alone," those Cedar Township believers reminded themselves again and again. Our God is with us! It made all the difference.

NOT AS ORPHANS

Jesus once told his disciples, *"I will not leave you as orphans; I will come to you"* (John 14:18). Even in a crowd, an orphan may not know safety, security. A toddler, left alone in the world by a sudden traffic accident or parental desertion or an act of terrorism, has no guarantee that any nearby adult will care, let alone help. In such a case, panic is a normal reaction.

The comfort in the name Immanuel comes from our Savior's pledge to act on our behalf and to be near us. Our Immanuel stands by us, not as a caseworker drowning in a sea of file folders, but as our friend. God is with us:

† As our confidante and companion.
† As our ally and helper.
† As our refuge and protector.
† As our comforter and guide.

Jesus comes, not to condemn, but to shelter and calm.

ONE IS THE LONELIEST NUMBER

When do the ghosts of loneliness haunt your heart? Some people experience loneliness in a crowded office, doing work they find meaningless or putting up with a supervisor who berates them. Some people feel lonely as they lie in bed next to a spouse who has become a stranger. Some people find themselves lonely as they grieve the miscarriage they can never quite forget or the relationship they never had or the career success that has always eluded them. All the songs have it right; one is the loneliest number.

From his cross, Jesus cried out in anguish, *"My God, my God, why have you forsaken me?"* (Matthew 27:46). The Son who had always known the embrace of the Father's love and the peace of the Father's presence became an orphan, abandoned by the Father so that you and I would never know God's abandonment, no matter how many times we break his commands. Instead, we have been adopted into God's family. Jesus endured the loneliness of separation from God so that we could live as sons and daughters of the King forever.

In Immanuel, we are never alone – no matter how we may feel at any given point. Jesus knows – genuinely knows – what loneliness is like. He will not leave us living like orphans; he has come to us and he keeps coming:

    † As we walk into that lonely office, we can picture him taking our hand and sitting beside us.

    † As tears of grief fill our eyes yet again, we can picture him holding us and crying with us.

    † As we attempt one more conversation with that estranged spouse, we can know the presence of our Savior, making his appeal for peace through us.

Despite all appearances, despite what we may so often feel, we are not alone. We are never alone. Our God is with us in the person of his Son, Jesus. Immanuel is his gift to us, and that gift makes all the difference.

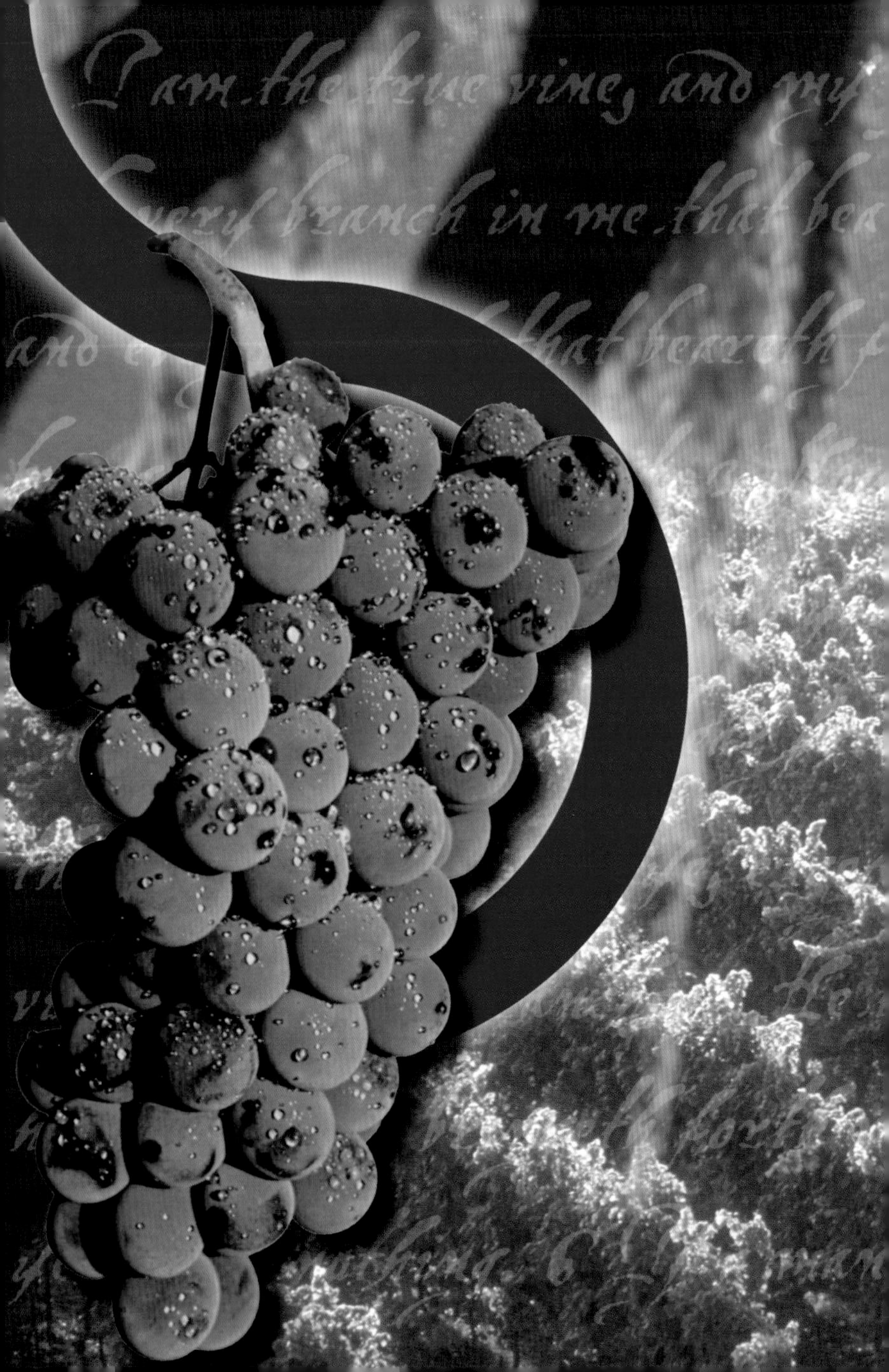
I am the true vine, and my
branch in me that

The VINE

JOHN 15:5

"I am the Vine," Jesus told his disciples shortly before his death. Perhaps you count this name of our Lord among your favorites. Many Christians do. The rich meaning embedded in this name inspires courage and strength in our hearts. (See John 15:1-17.)

INTIMACY

Does the idea of intimacy with God thrill you? Or send cold chills down your spine? Many who claim to be Christians consider intimacy with God threatening. They work hard to keep the Almighty at arm's length, perhaps filling their minds with intellectual religious theories or obscure spiritual speculations. Or they adopt the outward trappings of the faith without allowing the inner meaning to penetrate their hearts and touch their hurts. Always, though, they are avoiding, avoiding, avoiding an authentic encounter with their Savior.

The claim Christ makes to this name, the Vine, dismisses all sterile, standoffish positions held by the faithful. The Vine maintains an intimate connection, an intimate union, with each branch. We do not look to him for an occasional touch of grace. We realize that his life must continually sustain ours. We *"abide in [him] and he in us"* (John 15:4).

This abiding comes simply as we hear, read, learn, receive, and meditate on his Word, as we turn that Word over and over in our hearts, mining from it every nuance, every nugget of truth and blessing the Spirit has planted there for us.

A branch cannot connect itself to the Vine, nor can we keep ourselves connected. But as we continue to drink into our souls the spiritual nutrients available from the Vine, the life of Christ himself flows through us. We grow spiritually more viable, vigorous, and vital.

PRODUCTIVITY

The point of a vineyard is the fruit. No one plants grapevines hoping to grow a bumper crop of leaves! Likewise, Jesus focuses his followers' attention on fruit bearing in John 15:1-17. Here he uses the word *fruit* five times and *much fruit* twice more. The "leaves" of outward showiness are inconsequential. Some of our Lord's most frightening words center on this truth:

> *Not everyone who says to me, "Lord, Lord," will enter the kingdom of heaven, but the one who does the will of my Father who is in heaven. On that day many will say to me, "Lord, Lord, did we not prophesy in your name, and cast out demons in your name, and do many mighty works in your name?" And then will I declare to them, "I never knew you; depart from me, you workers of lawlessness."*
> ~ Matthew 7:21-23

Pause as you read the words *I never knew you*. Then shudder! We do well to take our Lord's warning to heart.

Still, no gardener stands in the vineyard scolding the branches for barrenness and berating them to produce a crop. Healthy branches simply do bear fruit. They can't help themselves.

Similarly, the branches connected to Jesus, the Vine, bear fruit – much fruit. This fruit just comes naturally, without any heroic effort on its bearer's part. Bearing fruit is what we do as a result of our connection to the Vine.

So what is this fruit? Scripture describes it:

> † *And it is my prayer that your love may abound more and more, with knowledge and all discernment, so that you may approve what is excellent, and so be pure and blameless for the day of Christ, filled with the fruit of righteousness that comes through Jesus Christ, to the glory and praise of God* (Philippians 1:9-11).

† *For the moment all discipline seems painful rather than pleasant, but later it yields the peaceful fruit of righteousness to those who have been trained by it* (Hebrews 12:11).

† *Walk as children of light (for the fruit of light is found in all that is good and right and true)…* (Ephesians 5:8).

† *But the fruit of the Spirit is love, joy, peace, patience, kindness, goodness, faithfulness, gentleness, self-control …* (Galatians 5:22-23).

Think of these passages as the pages of those seed catalogs that appear in your mailbox every February. Doesn't the aroma of their fruit almost waft off the paper? Doesn't the sweetness nearly melt in your mouth?

What a harvest! A bumper crop! But just as the promises made by each spring's seed catalogs often evaporate, leaving behind only disappointment, so, too, no branch will bear genuine fruit apart from the Vine. Jesus warns, "Apart from me, you can do nothing" (John 15:5). Not "a few things." Not "the easy things." Nothing!

So then, when we examine our lives for spiritual fruit and wish we had more, we need to remind ourselves that a focus on fruit will not help. Instead, we need to attend to our connection to Christ, to letting Christ's Word abide in us (John 15:7). Ask yourself, "When and how am I taking nourishment from the Scriptures?" The Word of God and only the Word of God nourishes and strengthens us.

MEANING

A sixth grade teacher asked a student to explain the difference between ignorance and apathy. The student's eyes twinkled as he replied, "I don't know and I don't care." Only a confirmed cynic, though, would declare his or her life meaningless and claim not to care.

Many have commented on meaninglessness as the curse of life in our post-industrial society. Boredom runs rampant, epidemic. Yet living connected to the Vine, bearing fruit in him, removes the possibility of meaninglessness from our lives – no matter when or where we live. When connected to Christ, growing in him, bearing fruit, more fruit, much fruit, we find life's one, true purpose. (See John 15: 2,5,8.)

What's more, as we come to see our own unmet needs for spiritual nutrients, we can count on Jesus' promise that "*If you abide in me, and my words abide in you, ask whatever you wish, and it will be done for you*" (John 15:7). As we continue to bear fruit, our lives honor our heavenly Father. We glorify him as we, in this way, prove to be Jesus' disciples (John 15:8).

Intimacy. Productivity. Meaning.

Our Lord Jesus has opened this path to every follower. Old or young. Poor or rich. Hourly wage earner or salaried professional. All of us, from every walk of life, each moment of our lives, have the fantastic opportunity to be connected to the Vine, the sustenance of life. What a gift!

HRIST
PSALM 45:7

"Tell us plainly," the high priest thundered, "Are you the Christ or not?"

"I am," Jesus answered.

When Jesus claimed this name, he sealed his fate. His execution was inevitable. (See Mark 14:53-64.)

Christ. The Anointed One. What made this name and Jesus' claim to it so provocative? Throughout Old Testament times, God anointed prophets, priests, and kings for service to his people. To serve well, these leaders needed more than mere human understanding and insight. They needed the kinds of courage and wisdom only the Holy Spirit could provide.

CHARISMATIC LEADERSHIP

Business schools today study "charismatic leadership." The term charismatic, itself built on the Greek root word, charism, means literally "gifted."When Israel's first king, Saul, was anointed, the Holy Spirit fell so fully upon him that history records Saul was "turned into another man" (1 Samuel 10:6).

In ancient Israel, no one person ever held all three offices. The prophets were seldom priests; the kings occasionally prophesied, but never held the office of prophet or priest, and the priests weren't kings. In Christ the Anointed One, however, all the authority and the responsibilities of these three offices come together.

As King David had foretold a thousand years before, Jesus – the Christ – was anointed, gifted by the Holy Spirit, well beyond any individual leader before or since (Psalm 45:6-7; Hebrews 1:8-9):

† As our Prophet, Jesus proclaims the truth of God. In particular, he admonishes, corrects, comforts, and encourages each of us individually through his Word (2 Timothy 3:15-16). He is the Faithful Witness (Revelation 1:5) whose Word is completely trustworthy, eternally true, and absolutely effective in producing the results he sends it out to work in our hearts and lives (Isaiah 55:11). We can read that Word and listen to it preached, confident that Christ will speak directly to our hearts as he has promised!

† As our great High Priest, Jesus offered himself up as the one, final, perfect sacrifice for our sin (Hebrews 9:24-26, 10:11-14). Now he stands at the Father's side, praying for his people – you and me. We can live in full confidence that this Priest's prayers on our behalf are always answered (Hebrews 4:15-16)!

† As our eternal King, Jesus governs all the events of earth for the good of his Church, his people. He appoints us as his ambassadors to extend his gracious rule into the hearts of more and more individuals for whom he died (Ephesians 1:20-22).

"LITTLE CHRISTS"

The resurrected Jesus ascended to the Father's right hand, in part so that he could send the Holy Spirit to indwell each of his followers. Just before his ascension he promised his disciples:

> *John baptized with water, but you will be baptized with the Holy Spirit not many days from now.*
> ~ Acts 1:5

On the day of Pentecost, 10 days after Christ's ascension, the Spirit fell with power, anointing the believers for their service in Christ's kingdom. Still today the Holy Spirit anoints Christ's followers for effective service in his name. Still today we need the courage and wisdom only God can give. Still today we need to be turned into new people – people of compassion, insight, and humility.

When God's Old Testament prophets, priests, and kings were anointed, the anointing oil symbolized the outpouring of the Spirit. As we contemplate the Baby of Bethlehem, the Christ foretold, we can remember his promise to anoint us, to make us like him – his "little Christs." How can we help but ask for the fullness of his gifts, so that we might better serve others as we serve him with all our heart, soul, mind, and strength?

Lord Christ, saturate us with the oil of your Spirit and set us ablaze with every gift and the zeal that serves you gladly!

Thus saith the LORD, th...

the LORD of hosts; I am...

beside me there is no god. ...

declare it, and set it in order fo...

people... the things that are...

...make a gray...

...ings shall not...

The Lord of Hosts

Isaiah 44:6

A damp stench rose from every cell in the dungeon, offending even the most insensitive nostrils. Chains cut into the prisoner's wrists and ankles; the floor, stone hard and cold made a poor bed. Still, he slept – slept like a baby, seemingly unperturbed by the fact that in the morning he would sleep the sleep of death. The warrant already signed, the prisoner's fate was sealed. He knew it. Still, he slept.

The guards, four of the garrison's best, must have wondered at their prisoner's peace. And they must have wondered, too, about the extreme measures the king had taken to keep him in custody. Chained hand and foot in the deepest part of the prison? What danger must this uneducated fisherman from the backward province of Galilee pose?

THE LORD SENT HIS ANGEL

Trusting the chains, the guards allowed themselves the little luxury of rest. They figured the fisherman was going nowhere. But the soldiers' sleep soon grew into stupor, descending like the thickest of woolen blankets, blinding their eyes to the light that burst with brilliance into the gloom of Peter's prison cell.

"Get up quickly!" The apostle heard an unfamiliar voice as pain stung his ribs and the chains fell from his wrists. "Get dressed. Put on your sandals. Then follow me."

His eyes heavy and his mind still foggy from sleep, Peter did as he was told. "A vision," he thought as the dungeon's iron gates swung silently open before him. Only as the night air filled his lungs did the truth come clear. "The Lord sent his angel and rescued me!" he told himself. Several years of further service lay ahead. (See Acts 12:6-19.)

THE COMMANDER OF
HEAVEN'S ARMY

What will be, will be. Fatalists resign themselves to the idea that whatever is destined to happen, will happen. Fate is blind, inscrutable, and inescapable. Or so the skeptics think.

Those who live under the rule of Jesus Christ know better. Our lives rest in his hands, hands that still bear the nail scars, the reminders of his love for us, his mercy toward us. He knows us by name! We are his! His compassion for each of us never fails. Never!

As Peter lay chained in Herod's deepest dungeon, the Lord Christ knew exactly what had happened to his disciple. This was no mistake, corrected when the Savior shook a miracle out of his sleeve. Jesus knew precisely what he would do, and he provided peace while Peter waited for him to do it. As with Daniel, as with the three Hebrew teens facing the fiery furnace, as with Peter, so our Lord deals with us. Far from being helpless to provide relief when we face our own times of anxiety or disappointment or danger, our King carries the title Lord of Hosts. He still commands the angel warriors of heaven, the mighty heavenly host:

The chariots of God are twice ten thousand,
  thousands upon thousands;
  the Lord is among them …
~ Psalm 68:17

*Then I looked, and I heard around the throne and the
living creatures and the elders the voice of many angels,
numbering myriads of myriads and thousands of
thousands, saying with a loud voice, "Worthy is the
Lamb who was slain, to receive power and wealth and
wisdom and might and honor and glory and blessing!"*
~ Revelation 5:11-12

Peter could sleep in peace, knowing that the Lord of Hosts, the
Commander of heaven's angel army stood guard. He could say
with the psalmist, "In peace I will both lie down and sleep; for
you alone, O LORD, make me dwell in safety" (Psalm 4:8).
Can you hear the testimony of Peter, of John, of Paul, of
thousands of Christ's brothers and sisters shouting their
encouragement to you down through the centuries?

*I am sure that neither death nor life, nor angels nor
rulers, nor things present nor things to come, nor
powers, nor height nor depth, nor anything else in all
creation, will be able to separate us from the love of
God in Christ Jesus our Lord.*
~ Romans 8:38-39

This boast belongs to you as God's gift! The Lord of Hosts is
with you – each and every day! Believe it! And sleep in peace.

...eyewitness authorship of the ... by its highly developed theol-... ary style. For instance, some of ... worked into highly effective ... on them (chs 5 and 6); and the ... long discourses of a spea... f personified Wisdom in the ...

...about Jesus not found in the ... d on a baptizing ministry (3... the note on 2, 13); that he ... and met serious opposition ... 7,8); and that he was put to ... 9). These events are not id... e development and editing ... d of much of the detail of the ... nt that the Johannine tra-... itness. Although tradition ... f Zebedee, most modern ... upport this.

...the narrative has been or-... at's theological purposes ... e synagogue of the day ... d to exalt their master tt... as was the Messiah, and ... religious belief and prac-... l purposes have impelled ... ere not so clear in the ... explicit emphasis on his ...

...rch produced bitter and ... ility toward Jesus of the ... o are combined and ... g from their father the ... God by rejecting Jesus, ... author of this gospel ... not inferior to men in ...

...the Christian community the woma... esented as a prototype of a futur... nce of the resurrection is a woman...

The final editing of the gospel ... comes probably dates from be... emphasis have been favored on the pla... rtant a location in Syria, perhap... ve suggested other places, includ...

The principal divisions of the r...

I. Prologue (1, 1-18)
II. The Book of Signs (1, 19—12, 5...
III. The Book of Glory (13, 1—20, 3...
IV. Epilogue: The Resurrection Ap...

1 PROLOGUE*

CHAPTER 1

¹ In the beginning* was the Word,
and the Word was with God,
and the Word was God.
² He was in the beginning with God.
³ All things came to be through him,
and without him nothing came to be.
What came to be ⁴ through him was life,
and this life was the light of the human race;
⁵ the light shines in the darkness,
and the darkness has not overcome it.*

⁶ A man named John was sent* from God. ⁷ He came for testimony, to testify to the light, so that all might believe through him. ⁸ He was not the light, but came to testify to the light. ⁹ The true light, which enlightens everyone, was coming into the world.

...of grace and truth. ¹⁵ John testified to him and cried out, saying, "This was he of whom I said, 'The one who is coming after me ranks ahead of me because he...'"

WORD
of GOD
JOHN 1:1

I give you my word. When someone says this to us, they usually mean to emphasize the trustworthiness of their promise. If they have proved reliable in the past, we tend to trust the promise they have made. We "take them at their word" without asking for additional proof such as a down payment or earnest money.

THE FAITHFUL WORD

Can we take God at his word? Can we trust him? Or must we ask for additional proof? As if in answer to that question, the apostle John begins his gospel by coining a new and unique name for our Lord Jesus: the Word (John 1:1). God has given us his Word – in Jesus Christ.

God's Word is no philosophical idea floating around in the mind of some distant Deity. No, this Word is a person – Jesus Christ himself. He has proved himself fully reliable and completely trustworthy. He is the "faithful and true witness" (Revelation 3:14), the Amen to every promise God has ever made (2 Corinthians 1:20). Jesus is God's final, eternal, creative, all-powerful Word to humanity.

Here is strong encouragement indeed! We can cling tightly to God's promises to us in Christ. We can run to him for help in every time of need, no matter what the need, for he is faithful to us and to his Word. The Word does not lie. He cannot lie (Hebrews 6:18)!

THE CREATIVE WORD

God has given us his Word. That Word sliced through the darkness at the very moment of creation with a mighty, "Let there be light!" (Genesis 1:3). Today's physicists study light, building whole careers on their attempts to understand it, yet the Word created it in an instant, a split second, and in creating it, created time itself! What wisdom he must have!

But even more wonderful than the creative power he unleashed on Earth's first week, the Word of God continuously re-creates sinful human beings. Day-by-day, moment-by-moment, the Lord Jesus continues to grant new birth to person after person who believes in the forgiveness he accomplished for us with his death.

This Word, the second Person of the Trinity, took on human flesh (John 1:14). True God from all eternity, he became a true man, a true human being with blood and bones and muscles just like ours!

- † Can you see his little baby hands, reaching up from the manger bed toward Mother Mary's smile?

- † Can you see his toddler hands, pulling his growing body upright for the first time beside father Joseph's workbench?

- † Can you see his adolescent hands, grasping the saw or hammer and learning to use these with quick, sure skill?

- † Can you see his healing hands reaching out to touch blind eyes, useless legs, and lifeless bodies – and restoring them to full health?

- † Can you see those same hands pulled taut, pierced by cruel nails, and hanging from a Roman cross?

God has given us his faithful Word. This Word was "made flesh" (John 1:14). The Word-made-flesh worked eternal salvation for us by the blood of his cross. His hands and his flesh, now raised to life and glorified, still bear the scars of the battle by which he won eternal life for us!

Standing face to face with this Word, all mere human words of wonder, of praise, of awe seem totally inadequate.

Thanks be to God for his inexpressible gift!
~ 2 Corinthians 9:15

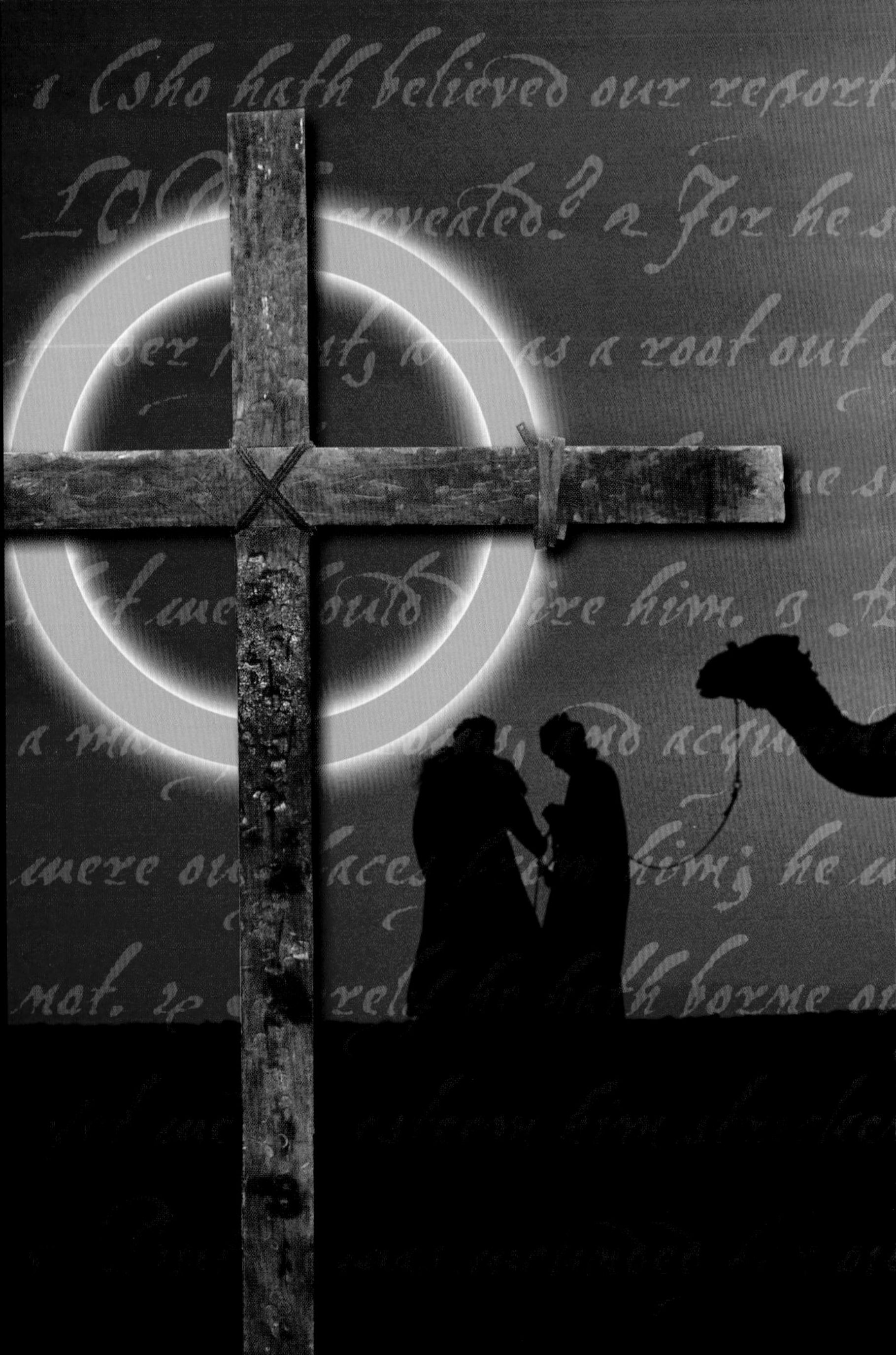
Who hath believed our report

MAN *of* SORROWS

ISAIAH 53:3

D id you ever have one of those "Three Dwarf Mornings"? You're Dopey, Sleepy, and Grumpy and, boy, do you need another cup of coffee!

All of us suffer through mornings like that once in awhile. Less common, but more troublesome, are those days or even weeks when we begin to believe we have a real, though invisible, target painted on our chest! Like some kind of colossal magnet, it seems to attract all the negative energy in the universe.

TARGETED

As the Lord Jesus walked along the paths of first century Palestine, he certainly could have imagined a perpetual target stamped on his robes. Consider some of the evidence:

† All four gospels report that the religious leaders of the day perpetually tried to trip Jesus by his words so they would have an excuse to arrest him. At one point, these leaders tried to stone him to death (John 8:59).

† The people of Jesus' own hometown, Nazareth, grew enraged with his teaching one Sabbath. They grabbed him and moved as a mob to throw him off a nearby cliff (Luke 4:28-30).

† Satan singled Jesus out for severe temptation in the wilderness as his earthly ministry began and again in the Garden of Gethsemane as his earthly ministry was ending. Based on Scripture, we can surmise that he faced many intense temptations every day in between. (See Hebrews 4:15.)

† The crowd that acclaimed him as its king when he entered Jerusalem on Palm Sunday became a fuming mob that screamed for his blood just a few days later.

No wonder Isaiah called Christ, the "Man of Sorrows." Still, all of this persecution pales in comparison to what happened on Mt. Calvary. There, Jesus became the target of God's infinite wrath. The Man of Sorrows carried on his innocent shoulders all of our sorrows, our grief, and our despair. He endured our pains and sicknesses (Isaiah 53:3).

Then, in his final hours and in a way that no finite human mind can begin to understand, our Lord suffered eternal separation from God – the agony of the damned in hell. Remember his words from the cross? *"My God, my God, why have you forsaken me?"* (Psalm 22:1; Matthew 27:46). The one who had lived in complete union with his Father from all eternity felt that union ripped away in condemnation for the sin he bore. Jesus hung on Calvary, fully alone, alone in a way he had never been alone, alone in a way that, because of him, we need never be alone.

In short, the Man of Sorrows suffered judgment for our wrongdoing, not his. Willingly, Jesus became a lightning rod, absorbing the wrath that our sins deserved. *"The LORD … laid on him the iniquity of us all"* (Isaiah 53:6).

JOY BEYOND ALL TELLING

The prophet Isaiah predicted more than sorrow for our Lord Jesus. After he described the agony of Jesus' soul, Isaiah added a note of triumph: *The will of the Lord shall prosper in his hand* (Isaiah 53:10). This, this was and is and always shall be God's will – our freedom from sin and death! Jesus made that freedom possible. Jesus brought into being what God had wanted from all eternity.

No longer the "Man of Sorrows," Jesus is now our Glorious King, and he shares with us the spoils of his victorious battle:

> *Blessed be the God and Father of our Lord Jesus Christ, who has blessed us in Christ with every spiritual blessing in the heavenly places, even as he chose us in him before the foundation of the world, that we should be holy and blameless before him...*
>
> *In him we have redemption through his blood, the forgiveness of our trespasses, according to the riches of his grace, which he lavished upon us, in all wisdom and insight...*
>
> *In him you also, when you heard the ... the gospel of your salvation, and believed in him, were sealed with the promised Holy Spirit, who is the guarantee of our inheritance until we acquire possession of it, to the praise of his glory.*
>
> ~ Ephesians 1:3-14, selected

Man of Sorrows ... Glorious King ... Praise him for his gift of victory!

Man of Sorrows! What a Name!

What a Name!

Man of Sorrows! What a name
For the Son of God who came
Ruined sinners to reclaim.
Hallelujah! What a Savior!

Bearing shame and scoffing rude,
In my place condemned he stood;
Sealed my pardon with his blood.
Hallelujah! What a Savior!

Lifted up was he to die;
"It is finished!" was his cry;
Now in heav'n exalted high.
Hallelujah! What a Savior!

When he comes, our glorious King,
All his ransomed home to bring,
Then anew his song we'll sing:
Hallelujah! What a Savior!

- Philip P. Bliss, 1875

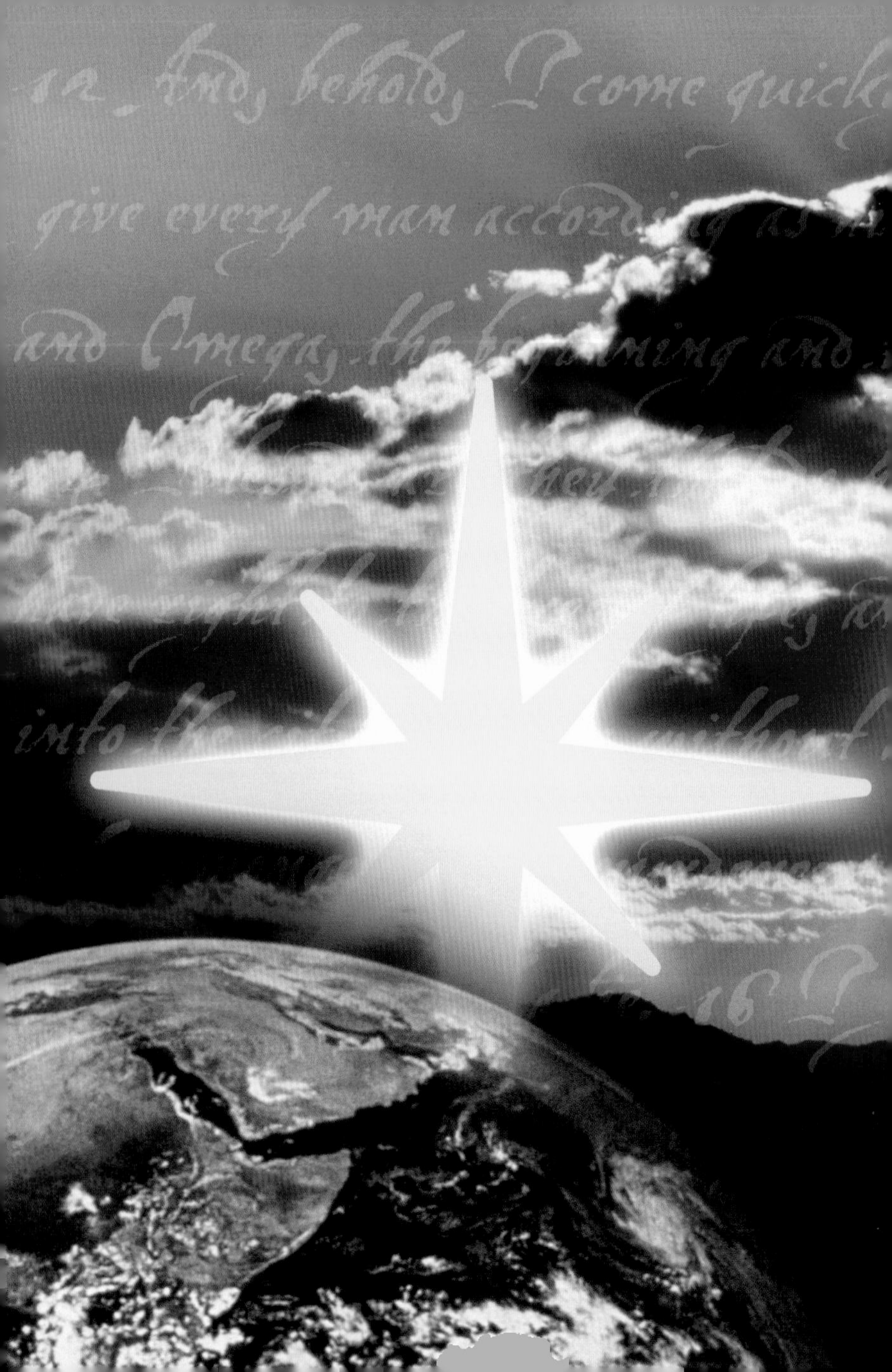
And, behold, I come
give every man
and Omega, the

BRIGHT morning STAR

REVELATION 22:14

Star power. It dances down the red-carpeted runways of Hollywood. It strides with prestige into the corner offices of Wall Street. It swaggers, sweating, into the locker rooms of every major city's stadium. And it floods those walkways, offices, and locker rooms with cash, boatloads of it! Fame. Influence. Power. Dollars. Star power attracts it all.

But the Hollywood stars, the financial stars, the athletic stars that prance across popular imagination cannot hold a candle to the Bright Morning Star who first came to earth, born in a barn to be our Savior.

One of Scripture's earliest promises about the Savior foretells his coming as the morning star – the "Star of Christmas," as it were:

A star shall come out of Jacob, and a scepter shall rise out of Israel;
~ Numbers 24:17

MALIGNANT DARKNESS

But why is the coming of the light such good news? In what way is the "star" of Christmas truly a gift from God? To understand that, we need to understand light's opposite – darkness.

In verse after verse, the Bible uses darkness as a metaphor for evil, for rebellion against God. Often, particularly in the New Testament letters, this darkness is portrayed as aggressive rather than passive. (For example, see Romans 13:12 or Ephesians 6:12.)

Matthew, Mark, Luke, and John follow suit. For instance, as Judas exits the Upper Room to betray Christ, John notes, "And it was night" (John 13:30). John does not drop this detail into the text so we readers can synchronize our sundials. Rather, he provides a commentary on the motives and intentions of Judas' heart.

Later that same evening, Jesus himself confronts his captors in Gethsemane with a stinging indictment: *"This is your hour, and the power of darkness"* (Luke 22:53). Again, the holy writer wasn't commenting on the absence of lanterns in the garden, but on the unseen warfare about to break loose in full fury on Calvary.

The darkness conspired against the Son of God and murdered him. That same darkness resides in all human hearts. Collectively, it causes the pain and suffering in our world. The Scriptures pronounce this verdict on all human beings: *"The light has come into the world, and people loved the darkness rather than the light because their deeds were evil"* (John 3:19). None of us wants to believe that about ourselves, but the Scripture is clear. We, too, add to the misery around us through our personal sin.

THE DAY STAR DAWNS

Into this cancerous and caustic darkness, a ray of hope burst in splendor. *"A star shall come out of Jacob,"* the prophet had promised (Numbers 24:17). And in first century Palestine, this Star set the sky ablaze with angels. Zechariah, father of John the Baptizer, recognized the hint of daybreak on the horizon:

> *Because of the tender mercy of our God, …*
> *the sunrise shall visit us from on high*
> *to give light to those who sit in darkness*
> *and in the shadow of death,*
> *to guide our feet into the way of peace.*
> ~ Luke 1:78-79

The Bright Morning Star scatters all darkness. In the eternal rule of our Lord Jesus, dark forces of evil will never again coalesce to distress us:

† The dangers and pain of this present, sinful world often threaten to terrorize our hearts. But today's dark terrors will not last forever. Our Morning Star is rising!

† Satan schemes to trip us into traps of habitual sin, plotting to torment us with the shame we bring on ourselves. But Satan's dark temptations will not last forever. Our Morning Star is rising!

† Dark thoughts and deeds haunt even Christian consciences with guilt as we reflect on our own daily disobedience. But the shadows of sin will not last forever. Our Morning Star is rising!

Not by accident, then, this Star blazes again from the pages of the Book of Revelation as the apostle John describes the eternal victory of our Lord at the end of time:

I [Jesus] am the root and the descendant of David, the bright morning star.
~ Revelation 22:16

Just think of it! The Savior who once claimed the title, *"Light of the world"* (John 8:12), will one day chase every scrap of darkness from the hearts of his people. The Bright Morning Star will shine into an endless day of peace, reigning resplendent in power. And we will reign with him, free from sin, free to soak in the light of his pure love, free to love our Lord and our brothers and sisters with a fervor we cannot even imagine now.

DAYSTAR IN MY HEART APPEAR!

This reality is the essence of what Jesus asked the Father to do in John 17. Jesus' prayer, offered up the night before he died for us, makes startling promises related to the glory of his bright love. Listen carefully to the words Jesus prayed:

The glory that you have given me, [Father], I have given to them [my followers], that they may be one even as we are one, I in them and you in me, that they may become perfectly one, so that the world may know that you sent me and loved them even as you loved me.
~ John 17:22-23

How much does the Father love the Son? That's the measure of the Father's love for you! And it's the measure of the love that will one day flow from your heart – your very own heart – toward your Savior and toward your brothers and sisters in the faith, your fellow citizens of heaven. It's an unwavering, immeasurable love!

Look again at the first part of John 17:22. The love of the Father for the Son and the Son for the Father is the glory of God – or at least its core dynamic. This love overflows in love for us, God's human creations. And Jesus proposes to share this glory with us – with each one of us, his followers. Even now, God floods his love into our hearts. Even now, the light of this love has begun to create the perfect unity in God's family that he has yearned to see from all eternity.

One day, we will experience this glory in all its fullness when the Bright Morning Star inaugurates the eternal Kingdom. This is Jesus' promise:

> *The one who conquers and who keeps my works until the end, to him … I will give … the morning star.*
> ~ Revelation 2:26, 28

Just as we are his, enfolded in his light and love, so he will be ours forever. No wonder that when the Wise Men saw the Christmas star heralding Christ's birth they "rejoiced exceedingly with great joy" (Matthew 2:10). Does that kind of joy overwhelm your heart today? It can. No matter what your challenges, they cannot keep the Star from shining. No matter how deep the guilt of your sin, it cannot extinguish the light of Christ's compassion and forgiveness. No matter how dark the future seems, your Morning Star has risen! Live in the joy of his splendor. It's his gift to you!

Wonderful Counselor, Prince of Pea...
Lion of Judah, Lamb of God, The G...
Sure Foundation, The Resurrection,
The Vine, Christ, The Lord of Host...
The Lord of God, Man of Sorrows,
Bright Morning Star, Wonderful C...
Prince of Peace, Lion of Judah, L...
Lamb of God, Sure Foundation, The
The Vine, Christ, The Lord of Hosts
The Lord of God, Man of Sorrows,
Morning Star, Wonderful Counselor,
Prince of Peace, Lion of Judah, L...
Lamb of God, The Good Shepherd, T...
The Wisdom of God, Sure Foundation...

...onderful Counselor, Prince of Peace,
...ion of Judah, Lamb of God, The God
...ure Foundation, The Resurrection, Th
...e Vine, Christ The Lord of Hosts,
...e Lord of God, Man of Sorrows, B
...Bright Morning Star, Wonderful Cou
...rince of Peace, Lion of Judah, Lam
...amb of God, Sure Foundation, The V
...e Vine, Crist, The Lord of Hosts,
...e Lord of God, Man of Sorrows, B
...orning Star, Wonderful Counselor,
...rince of Peace, Lion of Judah, Lar
...amb of God, The Good Shepherd, The
...he Wisdom of God, Sure Foundation,